UNFINISHED ANCIENT PROJECTS

Abandoned Due to a Worldwide Catastrophe

Front cover image by Shattered History.
Book design by Shattered History.

First printing edition 2023.

Visit https://www.youtube.com/@ShatteredHistory for more information.

UNFINISHED ANCIENT PROJECTS

SUDDENLY

Abandoned Due to a Worldwide Catastrophe

Shattered History

CONTENTS

INTRODUCTION

Ancient structures are often admired for their complex designs, enormous stature, and their durability to last over thousands of years. However, there are actually a surprising number of ancient projects (Fig. 1) which were abandoned before they could ever become as impressive as those which had been completed. Even some structures that are believed to have been finished show signs that they were planned to be far more elaborate. Given how much effort had already been put into these projects, it is very strange that they would have been left incomplete. Many of these structures have been damaged, some of which were damaged by earthquakes[1] and flooding. The sheer amount of unfinished structures across the world demonstrates that something may have occurred on a widespread scale which had prevented these buildings from being completed. In this book, we will be exploring these abandoned projects, and determining what may have caused these structures to have never been finished.

[1] Kázmér, Miklós, et al. "Damage to ancient buildings from earthquakes." *Encyclopedia of earthquake engineering* (2014): 500-506.

Fig. 1. The Unfinished Obelisk in Aswan, Egypt.

The Barabar Caves in India (Fig. 2) are a prime example of an elaborate project that was suddenly abandoned, despite all of the work that had been put into it. These megalithic structures were in the process of being carved from massive freestanding rocks.[2]

Fig. 2. Barabar Caves entrance.

---

[2] Dokras, U., Dokras, S. "Mirror-polished granite caves - Barabar Hills, South India." *ResearchGate*, 2020.

Many of the Barabar Caves' doorways are intricately carved (such as the door in Fig. 2), while others were left in an intermediate state as simple square doors with square frames cut out around them (Fig. 3). These square-cut doors are quite similar in appearance to carvings known as "false doors", which are carvings that resemble doors but are not functional entrances. While some false doors in ancient structures were created to be false doors, others are actually unfinished doorways, such as the one at Naupa Iglesia in Peru (Fig. 4), which was meant to become a functional doorway like the Barabar Caves' entrances.

Fig. 3. Barabar Caves entrance, India.   Fig. 4. Naupa Iglesia "false door", Peru.

Several of the rooms inside the Barabar Caves contain engravings which are believed to have been either false doors or shrines. However, there is evidence that these engravings were not finished being carved, and that they were intended to become functional doorways to connect the rooms inside the Barabar Caves. The walls around the door-shaped engravings are often polished, while the stone within the door frames has not been polished (Fig. 5). This indicates that the doors were going to be carved further in, as otherwise the builders would have polished the stone inside the door frames when they had polished the surrounding stone.

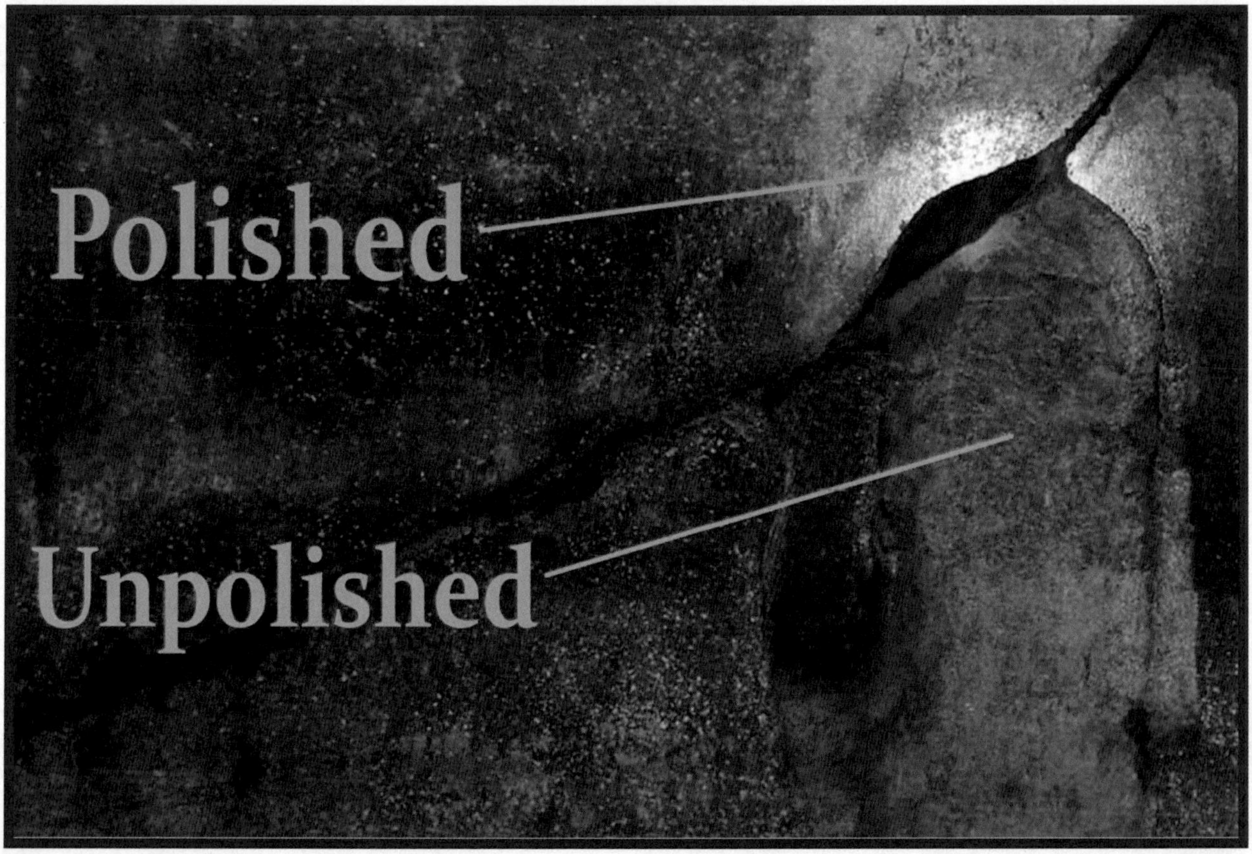

Fig. 5. Polished and unpolished stone inside the Barabar Caves.

Some interior sections within the Barabar Caves are highly refined and smooth, while other sections are still very rough and unfinished (Fig. 6). There are no carved bas-relief sculptures inside the Barabar Caves, which is very unusual, as most ancient buildings in India are covered inside and out with bas-relief sculptures.

Fig. 6. Unrefined, rough-walled interiors in the Barabar Caves (above), compared with rooms in the Barabar Caves which were highly-refined and polished (below), indicating that those which are not refined are unfinished.

By examining the unfinished sections of the Barabar Caves, one can see the processes by which the ancient builders refined their structures. In the Barabar Caves, it is apparent that the builders had carved and smoothed out the lower sections of the wall first, before refining the walls higher up towards the ceiling (Fig. 7). Only some sections are highly-polished (Fig. 8), while the other sections are unrefined.

Fig. 7. Unrefined and polished stone.   Fig. 8. Highly-polished stone.

The outside of the structure only contains a few lightly-carved designs, which were evidently intended to be more detailed and accompanied by many more carvings (Fig. 9). The exterior staircase had been meant to become more elaborate as well, but the stairs were never refined (Fig. 10).

Fig. 9. Unrefined engravings.

Fig. 10. Unrefined staircase.

There are enormous cracks running through the walls, primarily inside the structures (Fig. 11 (a) and 11 (b)) but also on the exteriors of the Barabar Caves. These cracks had been created by a strong force, such as an earthquake, which acted upon the buildings after they had been hollowed out.[3] It could be assumed that the reason why some of the interior walls were left unpolished is because the constructors had realized that there were cracks in the stone. If this were to be the case, then why were other interior walls, also with cracks in them, highly polished and refined? This is an indication that the cracks had formed after the builders had begun their work on the structures.

Fig. 11 (a). Cracks running through the walls inside the Barabar Caves.

---

[3] Khromovskikh, V. S. "Determination of magnitudes of ancient earthquakes from dimensions of observed seismodislocations." *Tectonophysics* 166, no. 1 (1989): 269-280.

Fig. 11 (b). Large cracks inside of the Barabar Caves; note that this crack has displaced the top-left edge of the incompletely-carved door frame, evidencing that the crack was created after the engraving had been carved.

The Mahendravadi Temple in India is another unfinished ancient structure that was carved from a single large boulder. There are designs lightly etched into the stone, and the exterior was intended to be carved more thoroughly (Fig. 12 (a), 12 (b), 12 (c), 12 (d), 12 (e), and 12 (f)). However, these carvings, as well as the structure itself, were never finished.

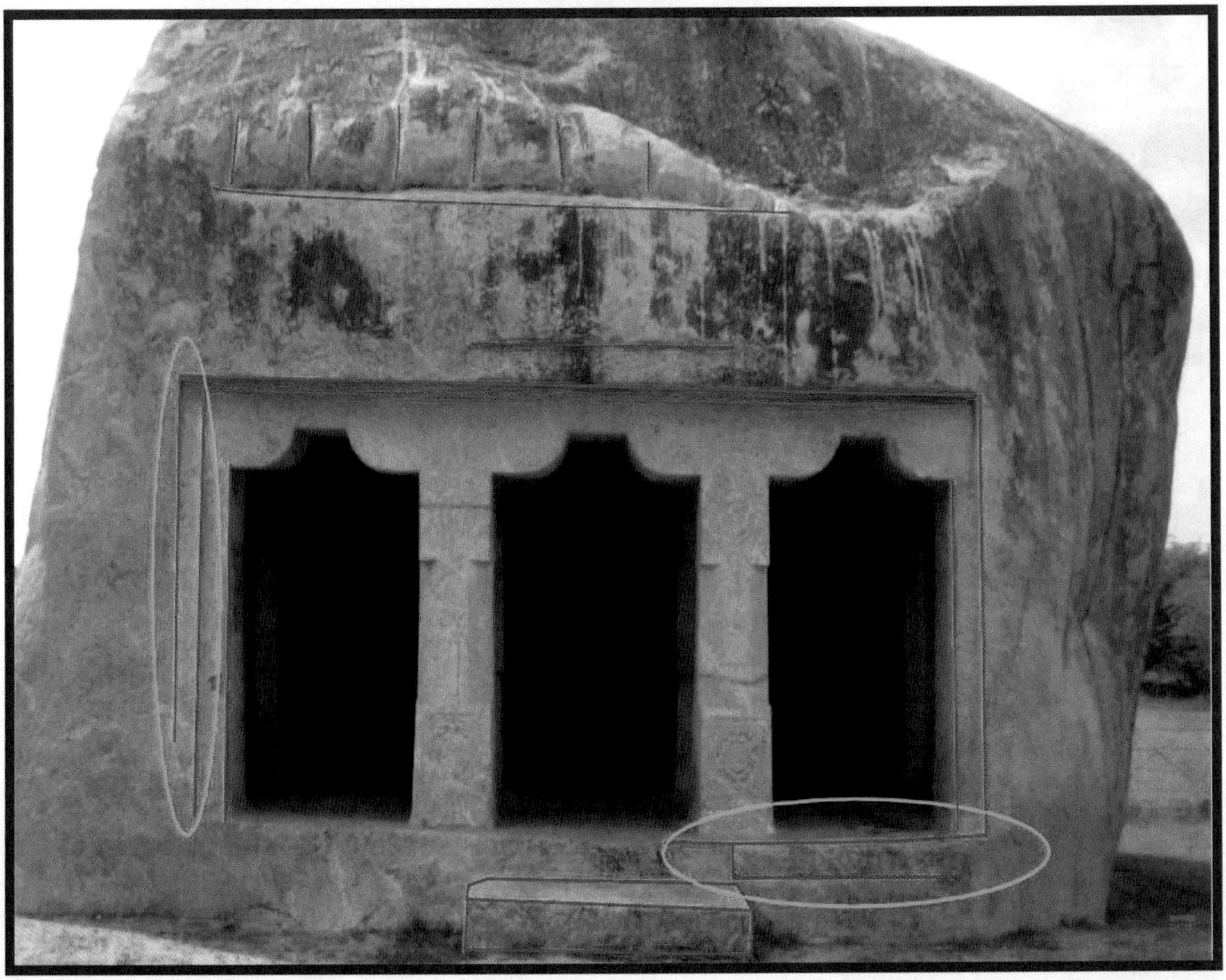

Fig. 12 (a). Mahendravadi; note the unfinished, asymmetrical carvings surrounding the entrance.

Based on the way in which many other structures in India (such as the Vettuvan Koil Temple, which will be discussed later) have been carved entirely from single masses of stone, it is very likely that the constructors had intended to carve the entire boulder to transform the Mahendravadi Temple into a freestanding, elaborate building.

Fig. 12 (b). Unfinished carvings on the exterior of Mahendravadi Temple.

Fig. 12 (c). Unfinished carvings on the exterior of Mahendravadi Temple.

Fig. 12 (d). Unfinished carvings on the exterior of Mahendravadi Temple.

18

Fig. 12 (e). Unfinished carvings on the exterior of Mahendravadi Temple.

Fig. 12 (f). Carvings inside of the Mahendravadi Temple.

Also in India, there are two separate cave complexes, Ellora and Ajanta, which are roughly 62 miles (100 kilometers) apart. Both the Ellora and Ajanta Caves contain many sections with few to no carvings or refinement where it seems that there should be carvings and refinement (Fig. 13). While designs are carved on many of the pillars in the Ajanta Caves, there are very few designs on the pillars inside the Ellora Caves (Fig. 14 (a), 14 (b), 14 (c), 14 (d), 14 (e) and 14 (f)). Although the Ajanta Caves are more elaborately designed than the Ellora Caves, neither of these structures are completed.[4]

Fig. 13. Refined and unrefined exterior of the Ellora Caves.

---

[4] Agrawal, Akanksha, Megha Naidu, and Ravindra Patnayaka. "Ajanta Caves: A Perspective on Construction Methods and Techniques." *International Journal of Research in Engineering and Technology* 5, no. 9 (2016): 217-223.

Fig. 14 (a). Ellora Caves exterior, unrefined and refined sections.

Fig. 14 (b). Ajanta Caves exterior, more refined than the Ellora Caves exterior.

Fig. 14 (c). Ellora Caves interior, uncarved pillars.

Fig. 14 (d). Ajanta Caves interior, carved pillars.

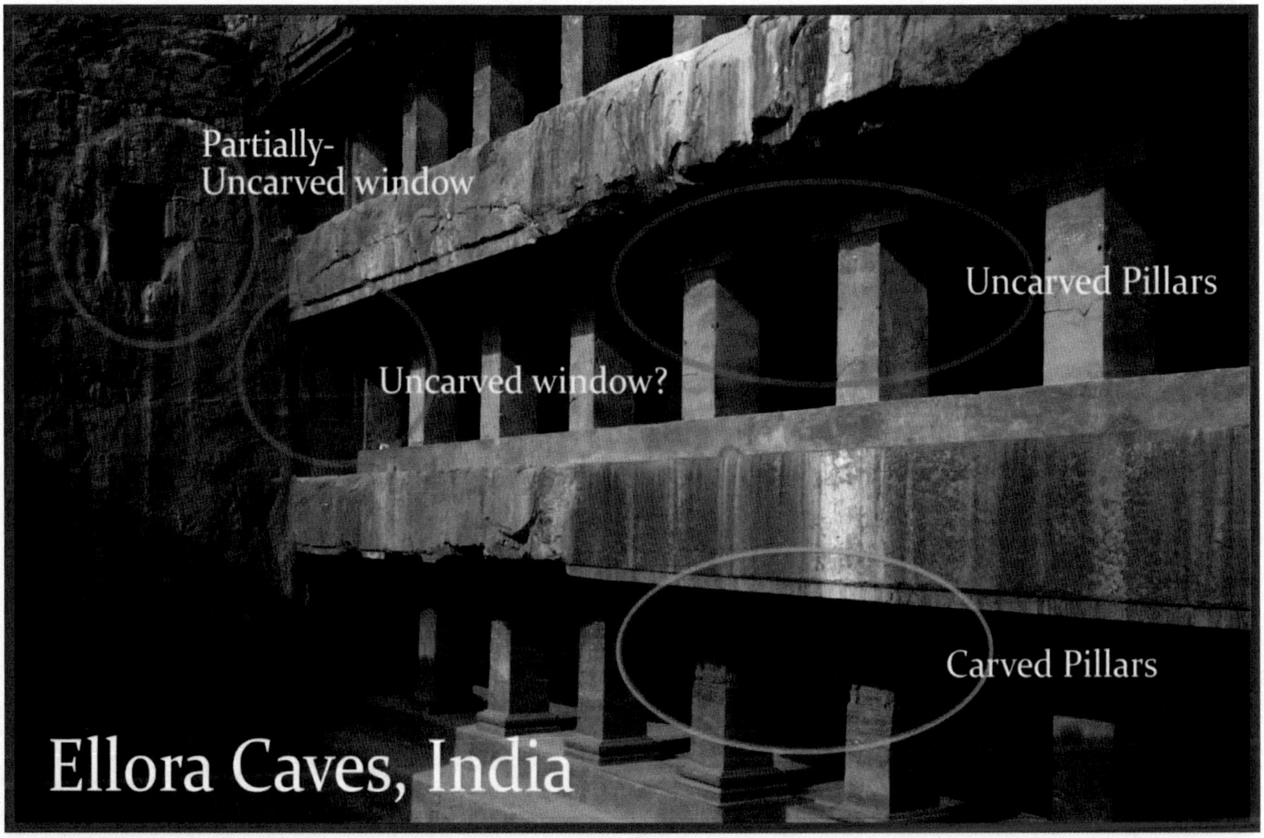

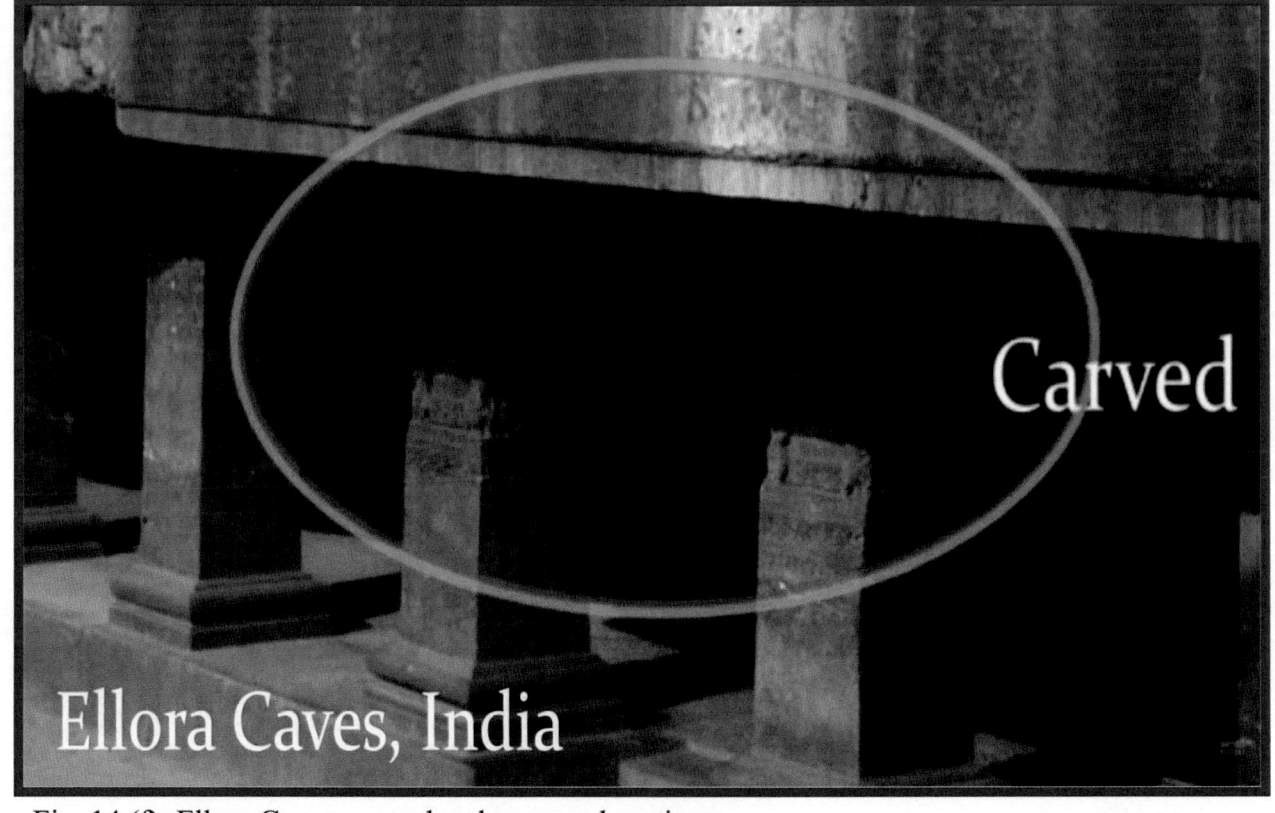

Fig. 14 (e). Ellora Caves, carved and uncarved sections.

Fig. 14 (f). Ellora Caves, carved and uncarved sections.

It is clear that there were plans for the Ellora Caves to be thoroughly designed like the neighboring Kailash Temple was, but the builders were never able to finish constructing and refining the Ellora Caves, nor the Ajanta Caves (Fig. 15 (a), 15 (b), and 15 (c)). Very few of the exterior pillars on the Ellora Caves have any carvings, which is unusual for ancient structures in India.[5]

Fig. 15 (a). Ellora Caves exterior (on left side of image), with Kailash Temple exterior (on right side of image).

---

[5] Dhavalikar, Madhukar Kešav. "Kailasa—The Stylistic Development and Chronology." *Bulletin of the Deccan College Research Institute* 41 (1982): 33-45.

Fig. 15 (b). Ajanta Caves, refined interior section.

Fig. 15 (c). Ajanta Caves, unfinished interior section.

VETTUVAN KOIL, INDIA

Vettuvan Koil is an ancient temple in India that was created in the same way that the more well-known Kailash Temple was built, having been carved out of a solid mass of stone. Unlike the Kailash Temple, Vettuvan Koil was never finished, however. A significant portion of the exterior of Vettuvan Koil has been left only partially refined (Fig. 16 (a), Fig. 16 (b), and Fig. 16 (c)). Some sections of Vettuvan Koil are elaborately carved, while other sections are not carved at all (Fig. 16 (d) and 16 (e)). Vettuvan Koil was most likely carved from the top down. While some workers had continued to carve out the bottom section, other workers began designing the top part and the surrounding rock walls. This process would have resulted in the top section of Vettuvan Koil being more refined than the bottom, because more time had been spent on refining the top. Very few designs had been carved onto the lower sections of the exterior, as of the time when the builders had been forced to halt their project (Fig. 16 (f), 16 (g) and 16 (h)).

Fig. 16 (a). Vettuvan Koil - unrefined.

Fig. 16 (b). Kailash (Kailasa) Temple - refined.

Fig. 16 (c). Vettuvan Koil, front entrance.

Front Side of Vettuvan Koil

Refined

The surrounding wall was going to be designed more, also.

Unrefined

Back Side of Vettuvan Koil (Carved)

Fig. 16 (d). Front (unrefined) side of Vettuvan Koil, compared to the back (more-refined) side of the same structure.

Fig. 16 (e). Vettuvan Koil, unfinished carvings compared to the finished carvings on the Kailash (Kailasa) Temple.

Fig. 16 (f). Interior of Vettuvan Koil (unrefined and cracked like the Barabar Caves).

Fig. 16 (g). The stairs leading to the front entrance of Vettuvan Koil may have been crudely carved due to being only temporary stairs that were used until the builders could carve elaborate stairs (see bottom-left corner of figure for an example of modern temporary stairs for comparison).

Fig. 16 (h). Stairs leading to the entrance of finished ancient temples in India are ornate, level, and refined, on the other hand - further revealing the incomplete state of Vettuvan Koil (above is the Konark Temple in India).

EGYPTIAN PYRAMIDS

Egypt is also home to a remarkable amount of abandoned ancient projects, which are rarely discussed despite their interesting implications. One example is the Tomb of Queen Khentkaus I, also called the Khentkaus Tomb (Fig. 17 (a) and (b)). This structure consists of a small limestone base that would have rested beneath a pyramid, encased in large limestone blocks. The Khentkaus Tomb is more narrow than a typical Egyptian pyramid. Due to its smaller size, it should have been easier to build than most of the other pyramids in Egypt, yet it was never completed. The Khentkaus Tomb is situated right next to the three Great Pyramids of Giza, and it was even initially believed to be an unfinished fourth pyramid of Giza.

Fig. 17 (a). Khentkaus Tomb.

Fig. 17 (b). Carvings made onto the natural stone base of Khentkaus Tomb.

The base of the Khentkaus Tomb is a natural rock formation which the builders had taken advantage of. The constructors had been in the process of covering this outcropping with stone blocks, as of when the project was halted. Carvings were made into the natural stone base, possibly to help the stone block casing adhere to the surface (Fig. 18).

Fig. 18. Khentkaus Tomb - unfinished stone block casing around the naturally-formed outcropping used as a base.

The Pyramid of Baka, also known as the Unfinished Northern Pyramid of Zawyet el Aryan, is another pyramid in which only the foundation and the lower part of the structure had been completed (Fig. 19). The shafts and chambers intended to be constructed beneath the planned pyramid were never finished, with only the floor of the chamber having been constructed.

Fig. 19. Pyramid of Baka (Unfinished Northern Pyramid of Zawyet el Aryan).

Another unfinished pyramid at the complex of Zawyet el Aryan in Egypt is the Layer Pyramid (otherwise known as the Khaba Pyramid), which stands at only 56 feet, or 17 meters high (Fig. 20 (a) and 20 (b)). The Layer Pyramid is estimated to have been over 275 feet, or 84 meters tall if it had been finished. Based on the angle of slope, it seems to have been intended to become a step pyramid. There is a chamber below the pyramid, positioned 85 feet (26 meters) below ground level, which is very deep underground and would have taken a significant amount of effort to construct (Fig. 20 (c)). However, there is no sarcophagus inside the underground chamber, showing that the structure was never used as intended.[6]

Fig. 20 (a). Layer Pyramid (Khaba Pyramid) of Zawyet el Aryan, Egypt.

---

[6] Dodson, Aidan. "The Layer Pyramid of Zawiyet el-Aryan: its layout and context." *Journal of the American Research Center in Egypt* 37 (2000): 81-90.

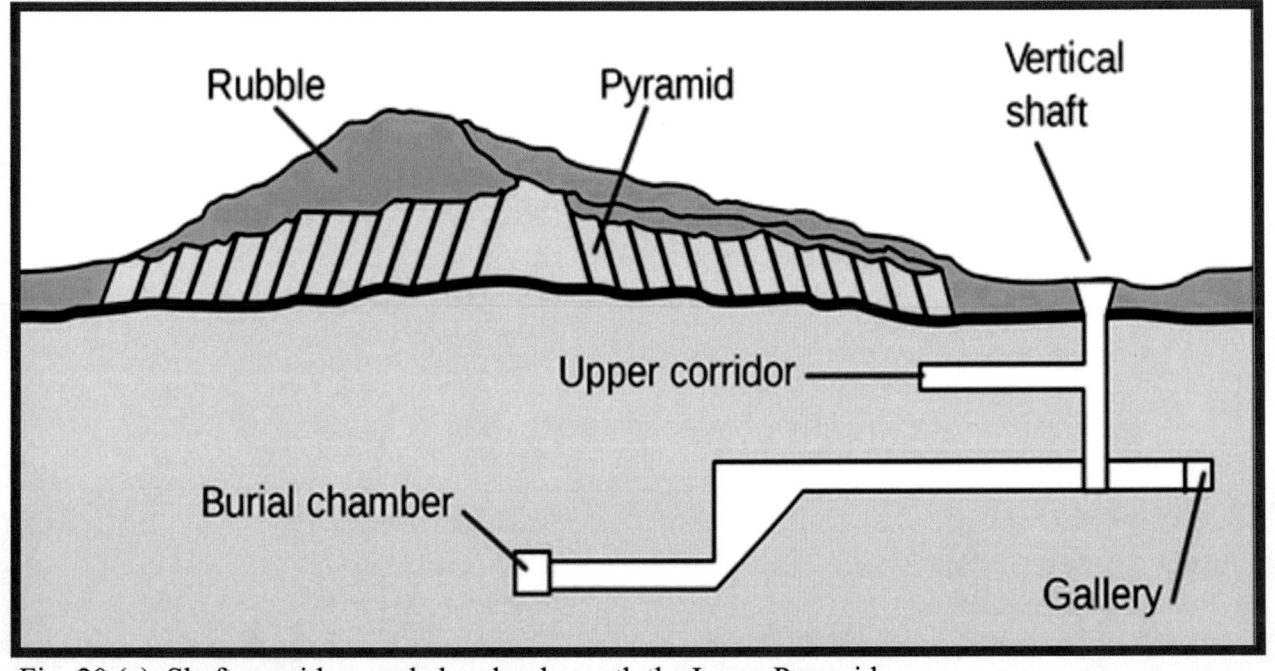

Fig. 20 (b). Layer Pyramid (Khaba Pyramid) of Zawyet el Aryan, Egypt.

Fig. 20 (c). Shaft, corridors and chamber beneath the Layer Pyramid.

A third unfinished pyramid at Zawyet el Aryan is the Pyramid of Djedefre (Fig. 21), which stands at only 34 feet (11.4 meters) tall now, but was apparently intended to be almost the same height as the Pyramid of Khufu (449 feet, or 137 meters) had it been completed.

Fig. 21. Pyramid of Djedefre at Zawyet el Aryan, Egypt

The Pyramid of Neferefre (Fig. 22 (a) and 22 (b)) is another unfinished structure that is a part of the Abusir Necropolis complex. The constructors of this would-be pyramid seemed to be in a hurry when attempting to build it, since only the outer layer was made of high-quality limestone, with the rest being made of low-grade limestone. This indicates that the constructors had resorted to gathering any limestone that they could find in an attempt to build the pyramid as quickly as possible.

Fig. 22 (a). Pyramid of Neferefre, Abusir Complex, Egypt.

Fig. 22 (b). Unrefined and partially-cut stone blocks found at the Pyramid of Neferefre.

According to Egyptologists, the Meidum Pyramid south of Cairo is another unfinished ancient structure in Egypt (Fig. 23 (a), 23 (b) and 23 (c)). It is still one of the most easily recognizable pyramids, since it was closer to completion than the unfinished structures mentioned previously. It has been claimed that the step-pyramid portion of Meidum was going to be covered in a smooth layer of bricks to turn it into a straight pyramid. It is currently 213 feet, or 65 meters high and would have been approximately 300 feet, or almost 92 meters high had its construction been completed.

Fig. 23 (a). Meidum Pyramid.

Fig. 23 (b). Interior of Meidum Pyramid - an ancient wooden support beam, remnant of unfinished construction.

Fig. 23 (c). Ancient wooden support beam inside the Meidum Pyramid.

The interior blocks in the Meidum Pyramid were unrefined, which indicates that they were cut into rough shapes, put into place inside the pyramid, and then other workers specialized in smoothing stone were planning on refining the blocks at some point (Fig. 24).[7]

Fig. 24 (a). Meidum Pyramid, unrefined interior blocks (lines added to highlight individual blocks of stone).

---

[7] Mendelssohn, Kurt. "A building disaster at the Meidum pyramid." *The Journal of Egyptian Archaeology* 59, no. 1 *(1973):* 60-71.

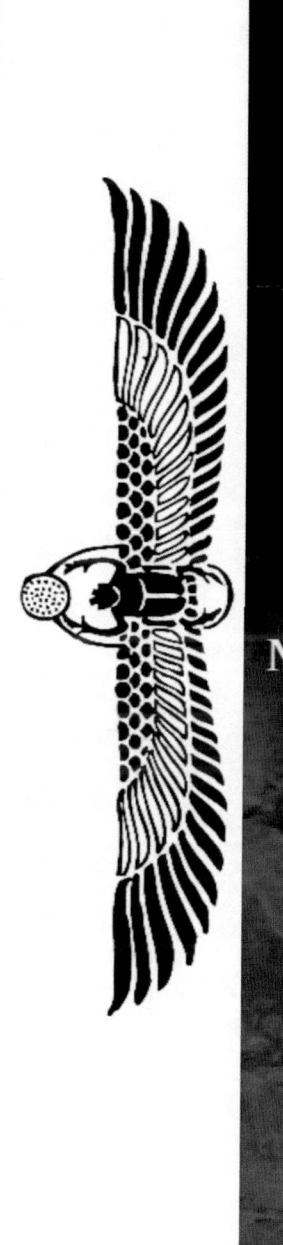

Great Pyramid of Giza Grand Gallery

Meidum Grand Gallery

Fig. 24 (b). Completed Grand Gallery in the Great Pyramid of Giza, compared with the unfinished Grand Gallery in the Meidum Pyramid.

43

YONAGUNI, JAPAN

An underwater megalithic site off the coast of a Japanese Island named Yonaguni also had been in the process of being carved for some purpose before it became submerged. The precise angles on the structure indicate that the stone had been carved by humans. Some claim that the structure is a building, and others believe that it is an ancient quarry. It is possible that this structure could have been both a building and a quarry. The stone may have been in the process of being cut away to become a building, and as the stone was carved, the constructors also took portions of the stone away to use in other structures nearby (Fig. 25 (a), 25 (b), 25 (c), and 25 (d)).

Fig. 25 (a). Yonaguni Monument.

Fig. 25 (b). Yonaguni Monument.

Fig. 25 (c). Modern quarry - note the similarities in appearance to Yonaguni Monument.

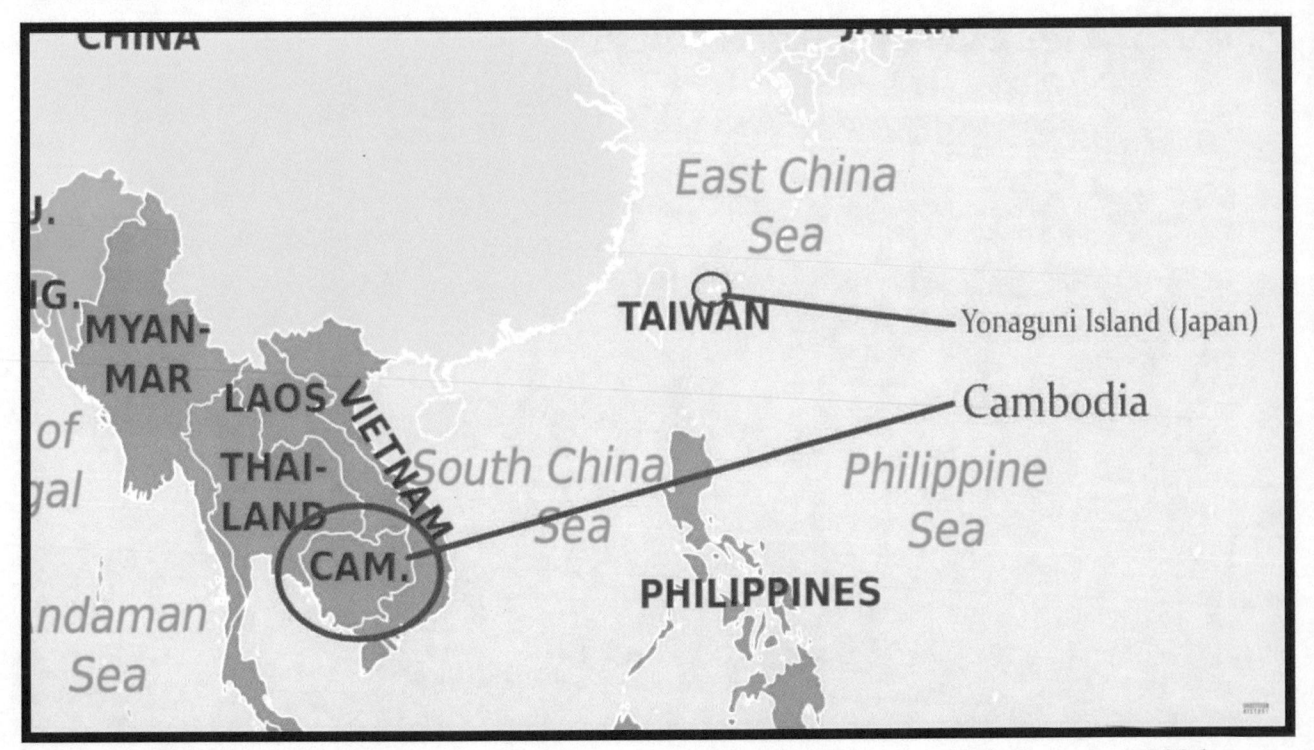

Fig. 25 (d). Yonaguni Monument.

Fig. 25 (e). Locations of Cambodia (Angkor Wat) and Yonaguni Island, which are over 2,000 km (1,242.7 miles) apart.

However, if the Yonaguni Monument had been a quarry, no other structures have been discovered in the vicinity that are made of the same type of stone. The closest ancient constructions that are made of the same type of rock are the structures of the Angkor complex in Cambodia (Fig. 25 (e) and 25 (f)), which still demonstrates that this type of rock was implemented in ancient construction projects.

Fig. 25 (f). Angkor Wat, Cambodia, made of black carbonaceous sandstone, the same type of rock that the Yonaguni Monument is composed of.

KAPILIKAYA, TURKEY

Another ancient structure that was abandoned before it was completed is known as Kapilikaya, where an enormous engraving erroneously believed to be a false door is carved into a mountainside in Turkey. The engraving is not actually a false door, but rather a giant, loaf-shaped block carved out from the mountainside. The megalithic block is still partially connected to the mountain, with the majority being cut away.

Fig. 26. Kapilikaya, an ancient structure in Turkey.

A gap was cut out around the Kapilikaya structure in order to prevent moisture from permeating through the stone of the mountain onto the structure.

Rocks are generally made of grains of minerals that have been cemented together by natural processes. The geometric and spatial configuration of the elements and minerals that form rocks, known as their "fabric", causes most varieties of rocks to be porous, making rock generally permeable by water as liquid is able to move through the connected pores in the stone (Fig. 27 (a)). Leaving the Kapilikaya structure connected to the mountain would enable moisture to pass through the rock composing the ridge and directly into the structure, permeating through the structure and weathering the stone (Fig. 27 (b) and 27 (c)). It would also cause layers of mold to form as moisture permeates into the chamber inside the structure.[8]

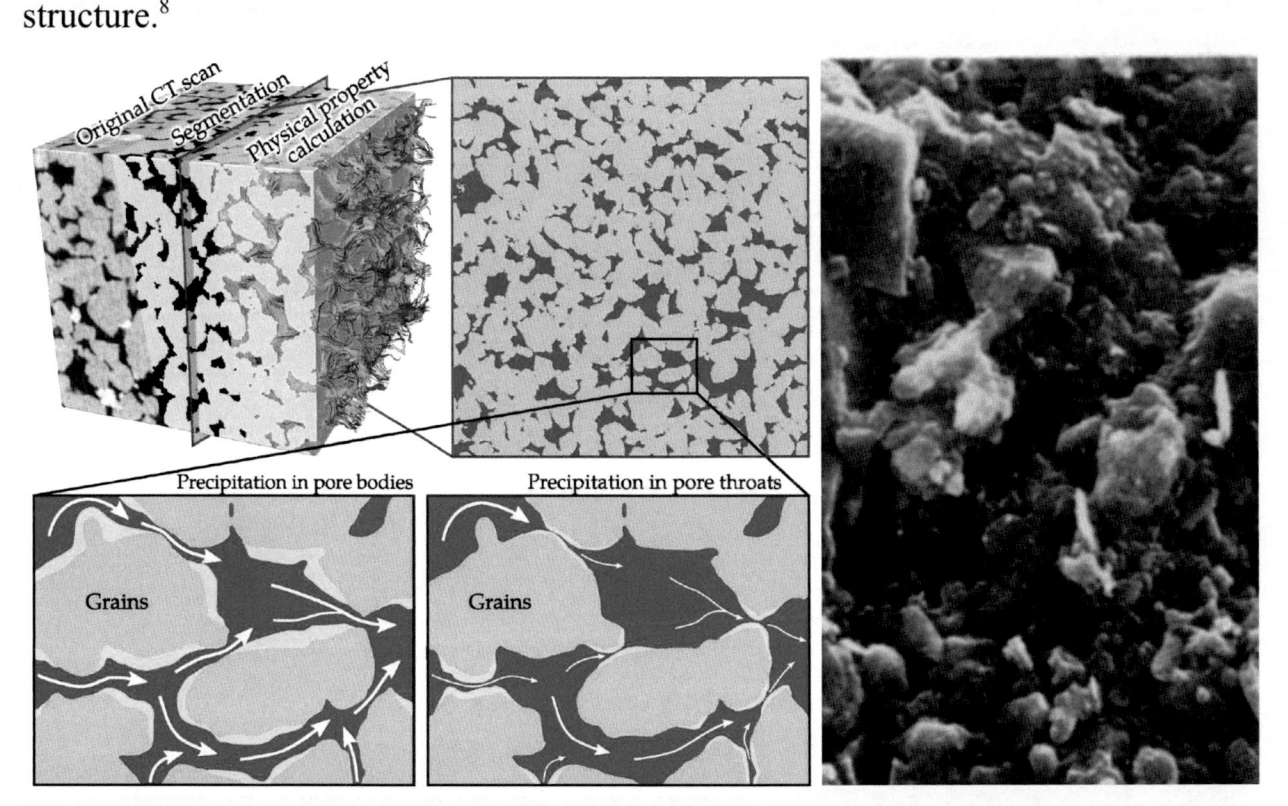

Fig. 27 (a). Rocks are generally porous, therefore water is able to seep through rock via the connected pore spaces (to the right is an electron micrograph of inorganic limestone).

[8] Erguler, Zeynal Abiddin. "Field-based experimental determination of the weathering rates of the Cappadocian tuffs." *Engineering Geology* 105, no. 3-4 (2009): 186-199.

Fig. 27 (b). Sections of rock were not carved, leaving the structure connected to the mountain and allowing moisture to seep through the connecting rock and into the structure.

Water slowly seeps through connected rock

Fig. 27 (c). Water can penetrate the structure through the connected rock.

The sections of stone around the structure that were not removed allowed water to seep onto the surface of the stone building. The uncarved portions around the structure are evidence that Kapilikaya was not finished (Fig. 28). The elevated rectangular cavity leading inside the structure was also not completely carved away.

There are 18 other structures of the same variety in Turkey, some of which are in different stages of completion, revealing what Kapilikaya was intended to look like (Fig. 29 (a)). There would have been an overhang on the building itself that would have shielded the rectangular opening from water, comparable to an overhang above a front door on a modern building (Fig. 29 (b)). The bottom edge of Kapilikaya was also designed to prevent water from collecting around the structure and to drain water away from the building (Fig. 29 (c)). The designs of Kapilikaya and the other ancient "rock tombs" in Turkey are quite ingenious, demonstrating that the ancient creators of the structures were very knowledgeable about how they could protect these buildings against water damage.[9]

Fig. 28. Other ancient "rock tombs" in Turkey which are more completed/refined compared to the Kapilikaya structure.

[9] Ince, Ismail, Mustafa Korkanc, and M. Ergün Hatır. "Evaluation of weathering effects due to surface and deep moisture in a Roman rock tomb: Lukianos Monument Konya (Turkey)." *Mediter Archaeol Archaeom* 20, no. 3 (2020): 121-133.

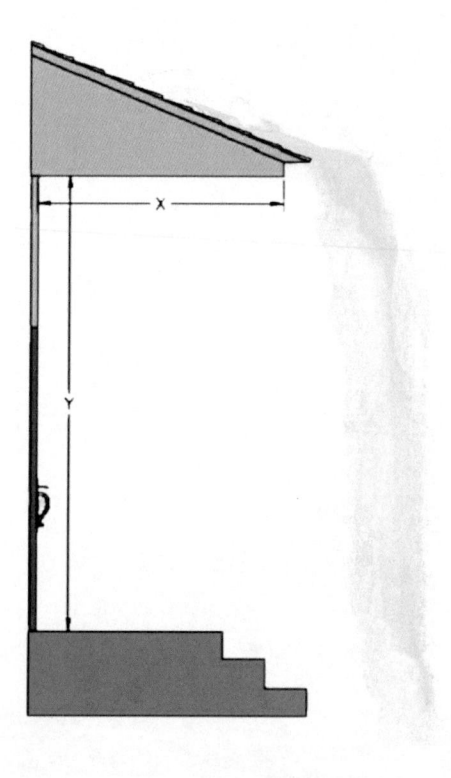

Fig. 29 (a). Other ancient "rock tombs" in Turkey which are more completed/refined compared to the Kapilikaya structure.

Fig. 29 (b). An overhang above a door redirects running water away from the entrance, and gutters guide stormwater off of the roof of a building.

Fig. 29 (c). Ground gutters for water drainage are carved around both sides of Kapilikaya to prevent water from collecting around the structure.

ARAMU MURU, PERU

A similar structure called Aramu Muru (Fig. 30), located in Peru, consists of a large rectangular outline carved around a smaller, T-shaped cutout resembling a doorway, which is carved into a natural cliffside. The frame carved around the structure would have served the same purpose as the frame around Kapilikaya, to protect the building from water damage.

Fig. 30. Aramu Muru, Peru

The doorway itself is cut in a very uneven manner, while the mantle higher up is more evenly cut, indicating that the structure as a whole was not finished (Fig. 31 (a) and 31 (b)). Modern people theorize that this site was created to be a shrine, hence the supposed false door, but that is only speculation with no real basis. The carving believed to be a false door was most likely intended to become a real door leading into a chamber, but it was never completed due to what appears to have been a major disaster that forced the project to be abandoned.

Fig. 31 (a). Asymmetrical carving of the architrave (mantle).

Fig. 31 (b). The frame of the uncarved door is uneven, with the top-left side of the door being further down than the top-right side. The mantle at the top of the structure, on the other hand, is completely level. The door would not have been carved to be crooked in its completed state, indicating that the door was not finished being carved.

NAUPA IGLESIA, PERU

Naupa Iglesia is another unfinished ancient structure that is located in Peru. Like Aramu Muru, Naupa Iglesia contains a cutout believed to be either a false door or a shrine (Fig. 32). However, these supposed false doors were most likely intended to become functional entrances that led into rooms, but the builders never finished the construction. Ancient builders would have intended Naupa Iglesia to become a much larger building complex, but only the doorframes were carved into the stone before their construction was halted.

Fig. 32. Naupa Iglesia engraving, believed to be a false door.

The ancient man-made Longyou Caves in China were also left in an incomplete state of construction. The walls were in the process of being smoothed out after they were carved. Some sections are much more leveled out than others, indicating that the constructors had intended to eventually smooth out all of the walls (Fig. 33 (a) and 33 (b)). The Longyou Caves had become completely flooded in the ancient past (Fig. 34), and they were unable to be explored until the water was pumped out in 1992.[10] None of the depictions on the walls are ancient, as the art was added to the walls in modern times to attract tourists (Fig. 35).

Fig. 33 (a). Longyou Caves in China.

---

[10] Bing, X. U., and Zhang, Q. "Analysis of the engineering geological conditions of Longyou stone caves and primary study on the protection strategies." 工程地质学报 8, no. 3 (2000): 291-295.

Fig. 33 (b). Varying degrees of refinement visible in the carved stone inside the Longyou Caves.

Fig. 34. Flooded entrance to the Longyou Caves.

Fig. 35 (a). Recently-made (not ancient) artistic reliefs on the walls and pillars in the ancient Longyou Caves.

LYCIAN ROCK TOMBS, TURKEY

The Lycian Rock Tombs (Fig. 36 (a)) are another set of ancient buildings that have been carved into the sides of mountains in Turkey, which is the same modern-day country that the Kapilikaya ancient structure is located in. Most of the Lycian Rock Tombs also have gaps cut out around them to prevent water from permeating them from the mountainside. The indentations surrounding the less-finished structures were evidently going to be carved more thoroughly to match the depth of the indentations surrounding those which were closer to being completed (Fig. 36 (b) and 36 (c)).

Fig. 36 (a). Lycian Rock Tombs, Turkey.

Fig. 36 (b). Varying depths of the stone carved out surrounding the structures.

Fig. 36 (c). Unfinished bottom portion of a Lycian ancient cliffside building.

The Lycian Rock Tombs are recessed into the mountainside, in the same way that RVs are parked into garages to protect them from the elements (Fig. 37). The largest building section of the Lycian Rock Tombs was never finished being carved, as only the top portion was designed, and there is no doorway. The lack of refinement is not solely due to erosion, because the other sections are still finely detailed. There were evidently plans to finish carving these buildings and to make them functional and accessible, but despite all of the effort that was put into them, their construction was never completed.

Fig. 37. The Lycian Rock Tombs are recessed into the mountainside, in the same way that RVs are parked into garages to protect them from the elements.

HEGRA CITY (MADA'IN SALIH), SAUDI ARABIA

Large palace-like buildings forming what is known as the Hegra City, or Mada'in Salih, were carved into natural buttes in Saudi Arabia. Several of the buildings of Hegra City were clearly unfinished, as only the top portions of these structures had been carved, and some have no entrances (Fig. 38 (a), 38 (b) and 38 (c)).

Fig. 38 (a). Hegra City (Mada'in Salih) in Saudi Arabia.

Fig. 38 (b). Unfinished ancient buildings of Hegra City, Saudi Arabia.

Fig. 38 (c). Ancient buildings of Hegra City, Saudi Arabia.

Similar to the Lycian Rock Tombs in Turkey, there are ancient palace-like buildings carved into stone cliffs in Jordan, which have been named collectively as Petra. Many of the buildings at Petra were never finished being carved, as evidenced mainly by the lack of refinement on the sides of the structures (Fig. 39 (a), 39 (b), 39 (c), 39 (d) and 39 (e)).[11]

Fig. 39 (a). An ancient building at the site of Petra in Jordan.

---

[11] Kennedy, Alexander Blackie William, and Harry St John Bridger Philby. "Petra: its history and monuments." *Country life,* 1925.

Fig. 39 (b). Petra ancient ruins.

Fig. 39 (c). Petra ancient ruins.

Fig. 39 (d). Petra ancient ruins.

Less Damaged

More Damaged

Fig. 39 (e). Significantly more erosion is present on the lower portions of the buildings, indicating flood damage.

The most prominent indication that the structures at Petra were unfinished can be found inside of the buildings (Fig. 40 (a), 40 (b), 40 (c), 40 (d) and 40 (e)). Despite the intricacy of the exteriors of most of the structures at Petra, the interiors are almost completely unrefined. There is evidence that there were plans to make the interiors more elaborate. The frames around some of the doorways are partially engraved with patterns, for example. These doorways were not finished being carved, however.

Fig. 40 (a). Unfinished doorways inside of Petra.

Fig. 40 (b). Unfinished steps at the base of the unfinished doorways.

Fig. 40 (c). Unrefined floor.

Fig. 40 (d). Possible flood sediment and debris inside Petra.

Fig. 40 (e). What Petra might look like if the interior was completed.

Apart from entire buildings which were never completed, there are also many ancient megaliths across the world that were never finished being carved for use in projects. One of the most well-known examples is the Unfinished Obelisk in Egypt (Fig. 41 (a) and 41 (b)). This large stone had been almost completely carved into shape, when the project was suddenly abandoned. It is claimed that the builders quit carving the obelisk because they had noticed that there was a crack in the stone. It is clear that the crack was made after the obelisk was carved however, since the builders had cut dotted lines into the stone, which cross through the crack (Fig. 41 (c) and 41 (d)).

Fig. 41 (a). Unfinished Obelisk of Aswan in Egypt, crack running through carved lines.

Fig. 41 (b). Unfinished Obelisk, full view.

Fig. 41 (c). Unfinished Obelisk, cracked portion of the stone.

Fig. 41 (d). Crack running through the line of drill holes.

The builders certainly would have noticed the crack as they were carving the dotted lines, if the crack had been present as they were carving the lines. This indicates that the crack was made by some stronger force acting upon the stone while it was in the process of being carved, rather than being present beforehand (Fig. 42 (a) and 42 (b)). The crack is not the reason why the construction of this obelisk was halted; whatever had created this crack is the reason why the builders were forced to halt their construction.[12]

There are many other ancient projects worldwide that were more refined, and yet they now contain comparably large cracks. Some of the walls inside of the previously-mentioned Barabar Caves in India were finely polished, but there are now cracks running through them (Fig. 43 (a)). If those cracks were present before the walls were polished, the builders would not have tried to polish the walls, because there would have already been major defects in the material. Even if the Unfinished Obelisk in Egypt was abandoned because the builders had realized that there was a crack in the rock (Fig. 43 (b)), they would have repurposed the portions of the megalith that they had already carved for another project, since it is not easy to carve stone.

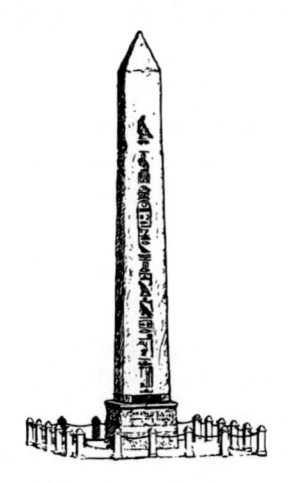

---

[12] El-Badry, et al. "Highlights on the Deterioration of Rock Art at Unfinished Obelisk Quarry in Aswan-Egypt." *International Journal of Multidisciplinary Studies in Architecture and Cultural Heritage* 2, no. 1 (2019): 67-104.

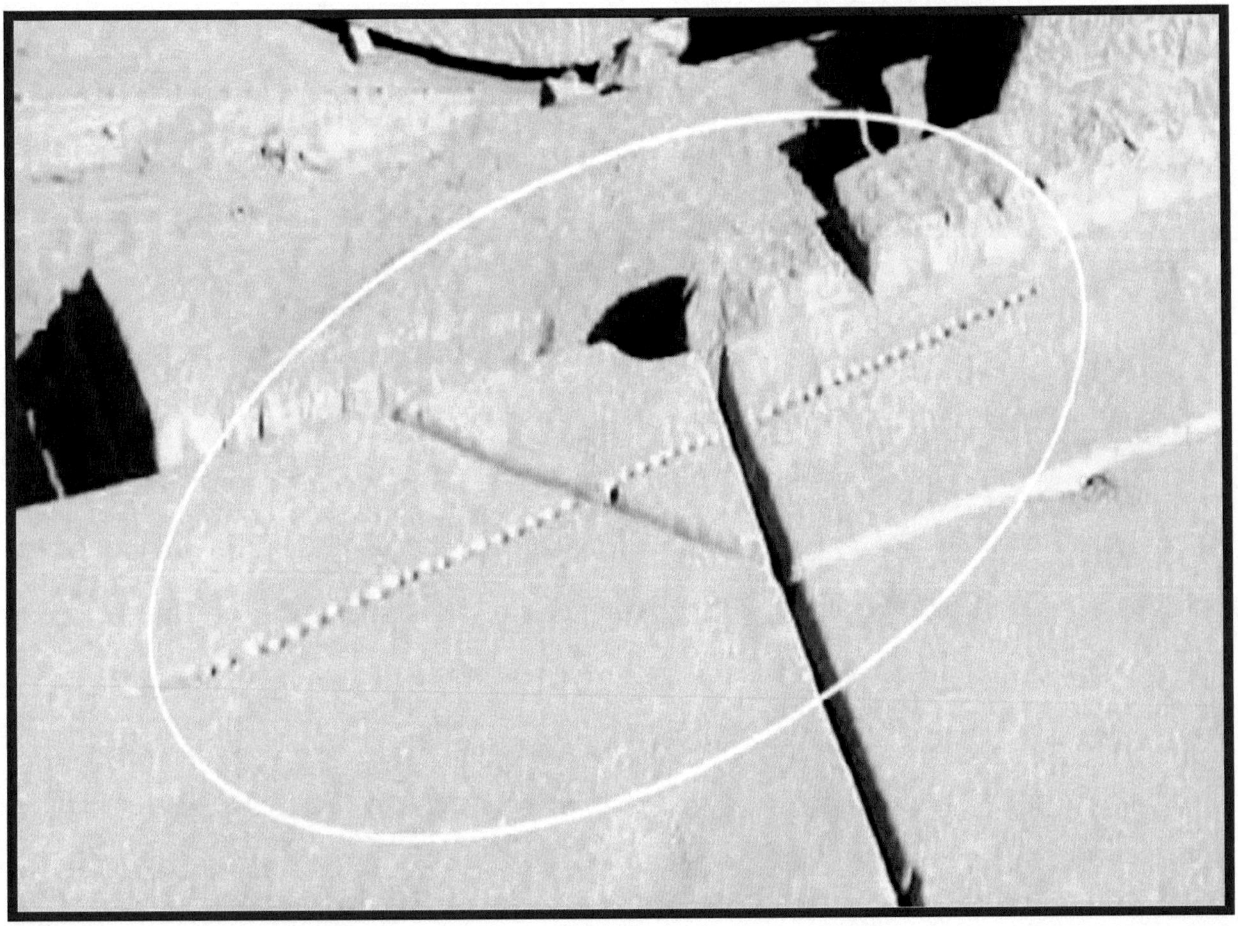

Fig. 42 (a) Crack running through the line of drill holes.

Fig. 42 (b) Crack running through the carved dashed line.

Fig. 43 (a) Barabar Caves in India - crack running through the refined wall.

Fig. 43 (b) Unfinished Obelisk in Egypt - crack running through the carved stone.

Fig. 43 (c). Unfinished Obelisk - partially-chiseled stone

STONE OF THE PREGNANT WOMAN AND OTHER MONOLITHS IN BAALBEK, LEBANON

There are ancient monoliths in Baalbek, Lebanon that were also in the process of being cut to use, most likely for a building that was never completed either. The most recognized of these monoliths is named the Stone of the Pregnant Woman (Fig. 44 (a), 44 (b), 44 (c) and 44 (d)), however there are several other unexcavated monoliths of a comparable size at Baalbek, Lebanon as well (Fig. 44 (e)). Although these monoliths do not have any apparent cracks in them, they were abandoned just like the Unfinished Obelisk in Egypt. It does not make sense that the ancient builders would spend so much time to carve these stones if they were not going to use them. There must have been some other factor which caused these monoliths to have been abandoned. These large blocks had also been buried when they were discovered, some entirely and others partially.[13]

Fig. 44 (a). Stone of the Pregnant Woman, ancient monolith in Baalbek, Lebanon measuring 20.76 meters, or 68 feet long.

---

[13] Abdul Massih, Jeanine. "The Megalithic Quarry of Baalbek: Sector III the Megaliths of Ḥajjar al-Ḥibla." *Journal of Eastern Mediterranean Archaeology & Heritage Studies* 3, no. 4 (2015): 313-329.

Fig. 44 (b). Baalbek monolith before full removal of sediment.

Fig. 44 (c). Stone of the Pregnant Woman, with other unexcavated megaliths below.

Fig. 44 (d). After removal of sediment covering the lower portion of the Stone of the Pregnant Woman.

Fig. 44 (e). The Forgotten Stone - another unexcavated monolith at Baalbek, Lebanon, measuring 19.6 meters (64.3 feet) long.

YANGSHAN QUARRY, CHINA

On an even larger scale than the other stone blocks discussed previously, there are enormous ancient megaliths at the Yangshan Quarry in China (Fig. 45 (a), 45 (b), 45 (c), 45 (d) and 45 (e)) which were clearly in the process of being excavated, but something had prevented those working on the excavation from finishing their task. The entire blocks of stone had been carved into shape, and all that remained was the separation of the megaliths from the ground. These enormous megaliths were abandoned before the separation process could be completed, however.[14]

Fig. 45 (a). A Yangshan Quarry megalith, as seen from above.

---

[14] Magli, Giulio. "A New Splendor." *Sacred Landscapes of Imperial China.* Springer, Cham, 2020. 99-114.

Fig. 45 (b). Yangshan Quarry megalith, with the base incompletely separated from the ground.

Fig. 45 (c). Yangshan Quarry megalith.

Fig. 45 (d). Beneath one of the Yangshan Quarry megaliths, showing the process of excavation which was never completed.

Fig. 45 (e). Northeastern section of the Yangshan Quarry - partially-excavated megaliths.

ISHI-NO-HODEN MEGALITH, JAPAN

In Japan, there is another large block of stone that was in the process of being shaped and excavated in the ancient past before the work on it was halted. This block, known as the Ishi-no-Hoden megalith, is carved into a cube-like shape, but with a unique pointed edge on one side (Fig. 46 (a), 46 (b), 46 (c) and 46 (d)). The top of Ishi-no-Hoden has been leveled, but debris has accumulated on top of it from the disaster that occurred in the ancient past (Fig. 47). According to Japanese legend, the construction of this stone was abandoned when there was rebellion against God, after which a catastrophe was sent in return.

Fig. 46 (a). Ishi-no-Hoden megalith.

Fig. 46 (b). Ishi-no-Hoden megalith.

Fig. 46 (c). Ishi-no-Hoden megalith, back view.

Fig. 46 (d). Debris on top of the Ishi-no-Hoden megalith.

The Ishi-no-Hoden megalith is also known as the "Floating Stone". This is because the edge around the bottom of the stone has been carved away from the ground, with only the center of the bottom remaining connected, giving the megalith the appearance of floating over the small pond it lies in. Ishi-no-Hoden was not cut into this shape so that it would appear as if it were floating, rather it was in the process of being carved and cut away from the ground to be used in a larger project elsewhere.

Fig. 47. Base of Ishi-no-Hoden.

There is another ancient megalith in Japan named Masuda-no-Iwafune. The original purpose of this stone remains unknown to this day, likely because it was never finished being carved and therefore it does not look the way that it was intended to. The bottom portion of the stone was still in the process of being carved away. It is clear that the builders were in the process of stripping away the stone, to smooth it out (Fig. 48 (a), 48 (b) and 48 (c)).[15]

Fig. 48 (a) Incomplete carving on the lower portion of Masuda-no-Iwafune.

---

[15] Kato, Hirokazu, et al. "Introductory Overview of Stone Heritages in Japan." *EGU General Assembly Conference Abstracts*. 2013.

Fig. 48 (b). Masuda-no-Iwafune megalith.

Fig. 48 (c). Note the similar carving methods used on the Mahendravadi Temple in India (above).

AL NASLAA ROCK, SAUDI ARABIA

Another megalith that seems to have been in the process of being carved, but was mysteriously abandoned, is the Al Naslaa Rock in Saudi Arabia. The center of the stone was split precisely in half. One side of the rock is completely smoothed out (Fig. 49 (a)), while the other side was left unrefined (Fig. 49 (b) and 49 (c)). The Al Naslaa Rock is similar to many other unfinished ancient stone projects across the world (including the aforementioned Ishi-no-Hoden megalith in Japan and the Yangshan Quarry megaliths in China) in that the perimeter of the base of each stone block has been carved away, with only a small point in the center keeping the stones attached to the ground. The fact that the ancient builders would have done this indicates that they were planning on separating the stone blocks from the ground and moving the megaliths to another location, but due to a worldwide disaster, each of these projects were cut short.

Fig. 49 (a). Al Naslaa Rock, Saudi Arabia - carved and smoothed-out side.

Fig. 49 (b). Al Naslaa Rock, Saudi Arabia - uncarved side.

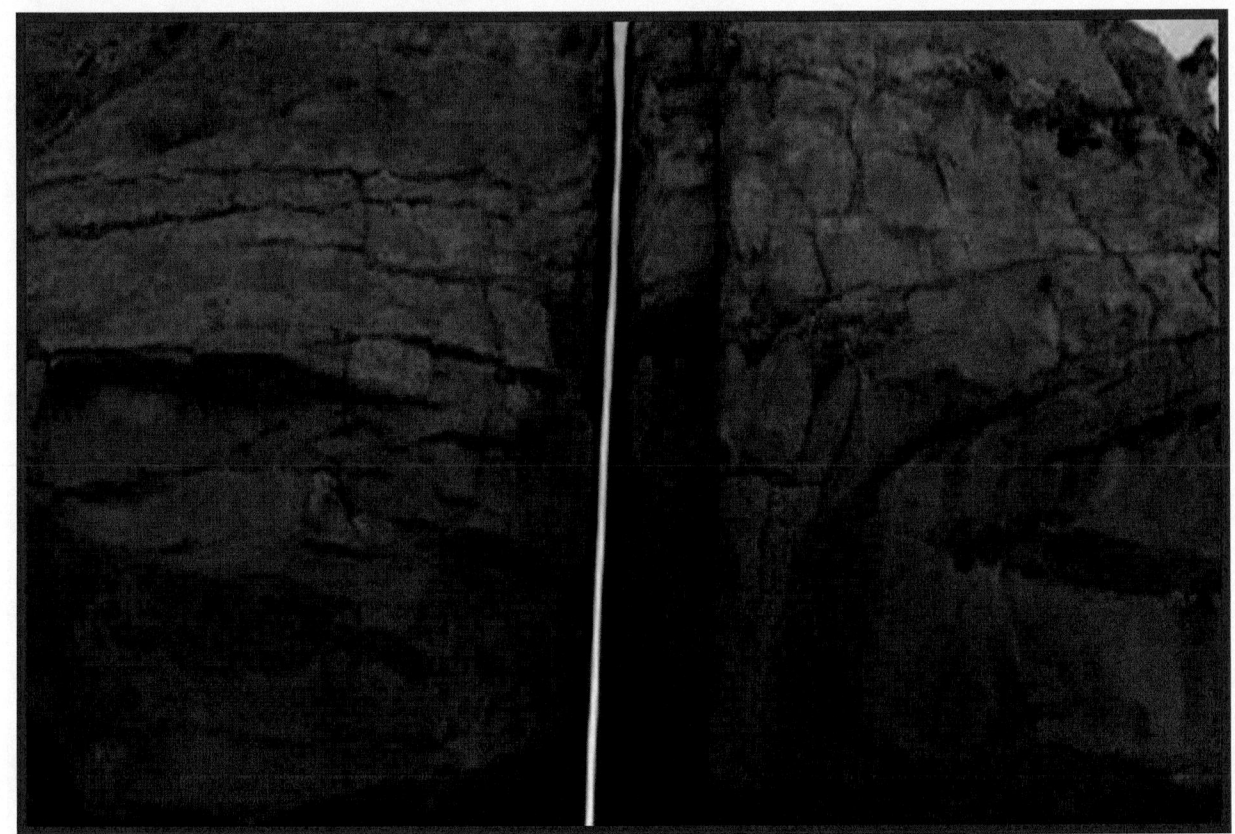

Fig. 49 (b). Al Naslaa Rock, Saudi Arabia - precisely-split rock.

94

UNFINISHED ANCIENT STATUES - MOAI ON EASTER ISLAND

Many ancient statues have also been discovered across the world which were never finished being constructed. Although there are almost one thousand completed Moai statues on Easter Island (Rapa Nui), there are a large number of Moai statues that are still only partially carved out from the rock and were never erected (Fig. 50 (a), 50 (b), 50 (c) and 50 (d)). There are no large cracks running through these Moai statues that mainstream archaeologists can use to explain why they were abandoned, as they attempted to do for the Unfinished Obelisk in Egypt.[16]

Fig. 50 (a). Unfinished Moai statues on Easter Island (Rapa Nui).

---

[16] Mulloy, William. "A speculative reconstruction of techniques of carving transporting and erecting Easter Island statues." *Archaeology & Physical Anthropology in Oceania* 5, no. 1 (1970): 1-23.

Fig. 50 (b). Unfinished Moai statues (same statues as Fig. 50 (a)).

Fig. 50 (c). Another unfinished Moai statue.

Fig. 50 (d). Unfinished Moai statue (same statue as Fig. 50 (c)).

There are many ancient stone statues in Egypt that were also left unfinished, and have been discovered in various conditions and degrees of completion (Fig. 51 (a) and 51 (b)).[17] What would cause these statues to be abandoned after so much work had already been put into them?

Fig. 51 (a) Ancient statues left in various stages of completion at the Pyramid of Djoser complex in Saqqara, Egypt.

---

[17] Connor, Simon. *Ancient Egyptian Statues: Their Many Lives and Deaths.* American University in Cairo Press, 2022.

Real Ancient Egyptian Statues, Found in Varying States of Completion.

Unfinished   Unfinished   Finished

Fig. 51 (b). Ancient Egyptian statues, unfinished and finished.

CONCLUSION

The way in which so many ancient projects across the world were abandoned and have remained unfinished for thousands of years is due to a massive, widespread catastrophe that occurred in the distant past. This major disaster forced the ancient builders to suddenly stop working on these projects, and they were unable to finish them later on. If there were only a small number of ancient projects across the world which had been abandoned, it could simply be due to localized events that drew the constructors' attention away from their projects. Since there are a multitude of buildings, statues, and megaliths across the world that had been suddenly halted in their completion, it indicates that something worldwide had occurred, separate from the unconvincing mainstream narratives that attempt to explain why these projects were deserted. The damage done to ancient structures indicates that massive earthquakes and flooding strong enough to damage stone structures and megaliths had occurred in the past, and that a series of disasters had happened after these projects had already been started. An astounding number of ancient texts from across the world describe a major disaster in the form of earthquakes and worldwide flooding which had occurred approximately 4,350 years ago. The evident damage that can be seen on many of these structures may be an indication that they are each remnants of a pre-cataclysmic supercivilization, and that these structures had been suddenly abandoned due to a worldwide catastrophe.

BIBLIOGRAPHY

Abdul Massih, Jeanine. "The Megalithic Quarry of Baalbek: Sector III the Megaliths of Ḥajjar al-Ḥibla." *Journal of Eastern Mediterranean Archaeology & Heritage Studies* 3, no. 4 (2015): 313-329.

Agrawal, Akanksha, Megha Naidu, and Ravindra Patnayaka. "Ajanta Caves: A Perspective on Construction Methods and Techniques." *International Journal of Research in Engineering and Technology* 5, no. 9 (2016): 217-223.

Bing, X. U., and Zhang, Q. "Analysis of the engineering geological conditions of Longyou stone caves and primary study on the protection strategies." 工程地质学报 8, no. 3 (2000): 291-295.

Connor, Simon. *Ancient Egyptian Statues: Their Many Lives and Deaths.* American University in Cairo Press, 2022.

Dhavalikar, Madhukar Kešav. "Kailasa—The Stylistic Development and Chronology." *Bulletin of the Deccan College Research Institute* 41 (1982): 33-45.

Dodson, A. "On the Date of the Unfinished Pyramid of Zawyet el-Aryan." *Discussions in Egyptology* 3 (1985): 21-23.

Dodson, Aidan. "The Layer Pyramid of Zawiyet el-Aryan: its layout and context." *Journal of the American Research Center in Egypt* 37 (2000): 81-90.

Dokras, U., Dokras, S. "Mirror-polished granite caves - Barabar Hills, South India." *ResearchGate*, 2020.

El-Badry, A., Abd El-Hakim, and Nasser G Abd El-Ghafour. "Highlights on the Deterioration of Rock Art at Unfinished Obelisk Quarry in Aswan-Egypt." *International Journal of Multidisciplinary Studies in Architecture and Cultural Heritage* 2, no. 1 (2019): 67-104.

Erguler, Zeynal Abiddin. "Field-based experimental determination of the weathering rates of the Cappadocian tuffs." *Engineering Geology* 105, no. 3-4 (2009): 186-199.

Fischer, Henry G. "An elusive shape within the fisted hands of Egyptian statues." *Metropolitan Museum Journal* 10 (1975): 9-21.

Hatami, Haleh, and Peter H. Gleick. "Conflicts over water in the myths, legends, and ancient history of the Middle East." *Environment: Science and Policy for Sustainable Development* 36, no. 3 (1994): 10-11.

Hoffmann, Friedhelm. "Measuring Egyptian Statues." (2002): 109-119.

Ince, Ismail, Mustafa Korkanc, and M. Ergün Hatır. "Evaluation of weathering effects due to surface and deep moisture in a Roman rock tomb: Lukianos Monument Konya (Turkey)." *Mediter Archaeol Archaeom* 20, no. 3 (2020): 121-133.

Kato, Hirokazu, Teruki Oikawa, Masayo Fujita, and Shunji Yokoyama. "Introductory Overview of Stone Heritages in Japan." In EGU General Assembly Conference Abstracts, pp. EGU2013-1641. 2013.

Kázmér, Miklós, M. Beer, E. Patelli, I. Kouigioumtzoglou, and I. S. K. Au. "Damage to ancient buildings from earthquakes." Encyclopedia of earthquake engineering (2014): 500-506.

Kennedy, Alexander Blackie William, and Harry St John Bridger Philby. "Petra: its history and monuments." *Country life,* 1925.

Khromovskikh, V. S. "Determination of magnitudes of ancient earthquakes from dimensions of observed seismodislocations." *Tectonophysics* 166, no. 1 (1989): 269-280.

Li, L. H., Z. F. Yang, Z. Q. Yue, and L. Q. Zhang. "Engineering geological characteristics, failure modes and protective measures of Longyou rock caverns of 2000 years old." Tunnelling and Underground Space Technology 24, no. 2 (2009): 190-207.

Magli, Giulio. "A New Splendor." *Sacred Landscapes of Imperial China.* Springer, Cham, 2020. 99-114.

Magli, Giulio. "Topography, astronomy and dynastic history in the alignments of the pyramid fields of the Old Kingdom." *arXiv preprint arXiv:0903.1416* (2009).

Mendelssohn, Kurt. "A building disaster at the Meidum pyramid." *The Journal of Egyptian Archaeology* 59, no. 1 *(1973):* 60-71.

Moses, Cherith, David Robinson, and John Barlow. "Methods for measuring rock surface weathering and erosion: A critical review." *Earth-Science Reviews* 135 (2014): 141-161.

Mulloy, William. "A speculative reconstruction of techniques of carving transporting and erecting Easter Island statues." *Archaeology & Physical Anthropology in Oceania* 5, no. 1 (1970): 1-23.

Pari Peña, Yenny. "Experiencias del turista energético sobre las frecuencias vibracionales emitidas del Portal Aramu Muru, Provincia de Chucuito–Puno, 2019." (2020).

Parr, Peter. "The architecture of Petra." *Palestine exploration quarterly* 128, no. 1 (1996): 63-70.

Qi, Yue Zhong, Li Lihui, Yang Zhifa, Lu Min, Xu Jianhong, and Zheng Jian. "An investigation on long-term stability and integrity of surrounding rocks in Longyou caverns caved 2000 years ago." In 11th ISRM Congress. OnePetro, 2007.

Rababeh, Shaher M. "How Petra was Built: An analysis of the construction techniques of the Nabataean freestanding buildings and rock-cut monuments in Petra, Jordan." *BAR Publishing,* 2005.

Raikes, R. L. "The physical evidence for Noah's Flood." *Iraq* 28, no. 1 (1966): 52-63.

Saleh, Mohsen M., et al. "Evaluation of geoenvironmental hazards at Qasr Al-Farid tomb, Mada'in Saleh, northwestern Saudi Arabia." *Arabian Journal of Geosciences* 14, no. 1 (2021): 1-14.

Singh, Virender. "Study of Indian rock-cut architecture." *ACADEMICIA: An International Multidisciplinary Research Journal* 11, no. 7 (2021): 167-172.

Sintubin, Manuel, ed. *Ancient earthquakes.* Vol. 471. Geological Society of America, 2010.

Stiros, Stathis C. "Identification of earthquakes from archaeological data: methodology, criteria and limitations." *Archaeoseismology* 7 (1996): 129-152.

Villeneuve, François, Daifallah Al-Talhi, and Laïla Nehmé. "Résultats préliminaires de la premiere campagne de fouille a Mada'in Salih en Arabie Saoudite." *Comptes rendus des séances de l'Académie des Inscriptions et Belles-Lettres* 152, no. 2 (2008): 651-691.

PHOTOGRAPHIC SOURCES

World History Encyclopedia
Page 68, 80

Metropolitan Museum of Art
Page 100

Wikimedia Foundation Commons
Pages 3, 7-9, 11-19, 21, 22, 24, 25, 27-38, 40-46, 48, 50, 52-54, 57-99, 100

ScienceDirect
Page 49

Pixabay
Pages 6, 9, 10, 11, 12, 13, 14, 16, 24, 26, 34, 35, 43, 52, 61, 63, 64, 67, 75

Shattered History
Pages 10-12, 15-17, 21, 23, 28, 29, 33, 36, 38, 39, 42, 46-48, 50, 52, 55, 56, 59, 60, 62-64, 68-71, 76, 81, 86, 89, 91, 99

INDEX

ABOUT SHATTERED HISTORY

The real history of our Earth has been shattered, and reassembled incorrectly, multiple times. The purpose of Shattered History is to correctly reconstruct history. Sometimes it's hard to experience a paradigm shift, but hopefully Shattered History's books and YouTube videos will help guide you through the shift we are currently experiencing.

Shattered History's YouTube channel:
https://www.youtube.com/@ShatteredHistory

Made in the USA
Middletown, DE
30 July 2024